SPORTS SUPERSTARS

LeBRON JAMES

BY KIERAN DOWNS

BELLWETHER MEDIA • MINNEAPOLIS, MN

TORQUE

Torque brims with excitement perfect for thrill-seekers of all kinds. Discover daring survival skills, explore uncharted worlds, and marvel at mighty engines and extreme sports. In *Torque* books, anything can happen. Are you ready?

This edition first published in 2023 by Bellwether Media, Inc.

No part of this publication may be reproduced in whole or in part without written permission of the publisher. For information regarding permission, write to Bellwether Media, Inc., Attention: Permissions Department, 6012 Blue Circle Drive, Minnetonka, MN 55343.

Library of Congress Cataloging-in-Publication Data

LC record for LeBron James available at: https://lccn.loc.gov/2022050057

Text copyright © 2023 by Bellwether Media, Inc. TORQUE and associated logos are trademarks and/or registered trademarks of Bellwether Media, Inc.

Editor: Rebecca Sabelko   Designer: Josh Brink

Printed in the United States of America, North Mankato, MN.

TABLE OF CONTENTS

SLAM DUNK!	4
WHO IS LeBRON JAMES?	6
A YOUNG STAR	8
THE KING	12
KING JAMES'S FUTURE	20
GLOSSARY	22
TO LEARN MORE	23
INDEX	24

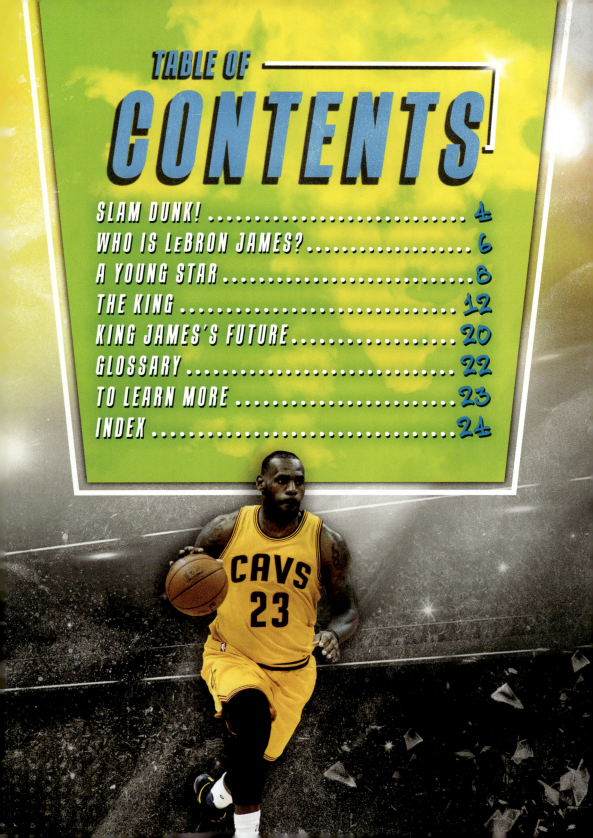

SLAM DUNK!

It is Game 6 of the 2020 **Finals**. LeBron James passes the ball to Alex Caruso. Caruso passes back to James. James drives the ball to the hoop for a **slam dunk**! The Los Angeles Lakers now lead by 32 points.

The Lakers win the game 106 to 93. LeBron James wins his fourth **championship**!

WHO IS LeBRON JAMES?

LeBron James is a **small forward** in the **National Basketball Association** (NBA). He has played for the Cleveland Cavaliers, the Miami Heat, and the Los Angeles Lakers. Some people believe he is the greatest basketball player of all time!

Major Moneymaker

In 2022, James became the first active NBA player to become a billionaire.

6

LeBRON JAMES

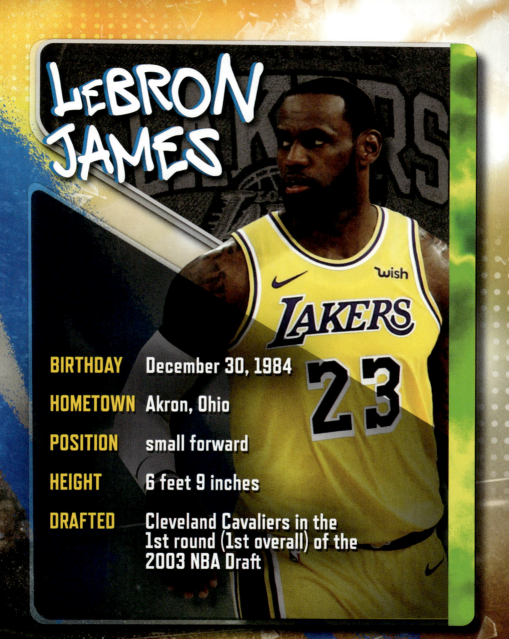

BIRTHDAY December 30, 1984

HOMETOWN Akron, Ohio

POSITION small forward

HEIGHT 6 feet 9 inches

DRAFTED Cleveland Cavaliers in the 1st round (1st overall) of the 2003 NBA Draft

James is also a successful businessman. He works with many companies. He is a **philanthropist**, too. He works to help people and communities.

A YOUNG STAR

James was a star basketball player at a young age. He led his team to state championships three out of his four years of high school.

James won many awards, too! He was named Ohio Mr. Basketball three times. He was the Gatorade National Player of the Year two years in a row.

James was chosen as the first overall pick of the 2003 NBA **Draft**. He was only 18 years old. He was picked by his hometown team, the Cleveland Cavaliers.

In his first year, James led the team in scoring, **steals**, and playing time. He won the NBA **Rookie** of the Year award.

2003 NBA DRAFT

A Big Deal

James signed a $90 million deal from Nike before he even played an NBA game!

FAVORITES

PET	FOOD	COLOR	CARTOON
dog	turkey	blue	Tom and Jerry

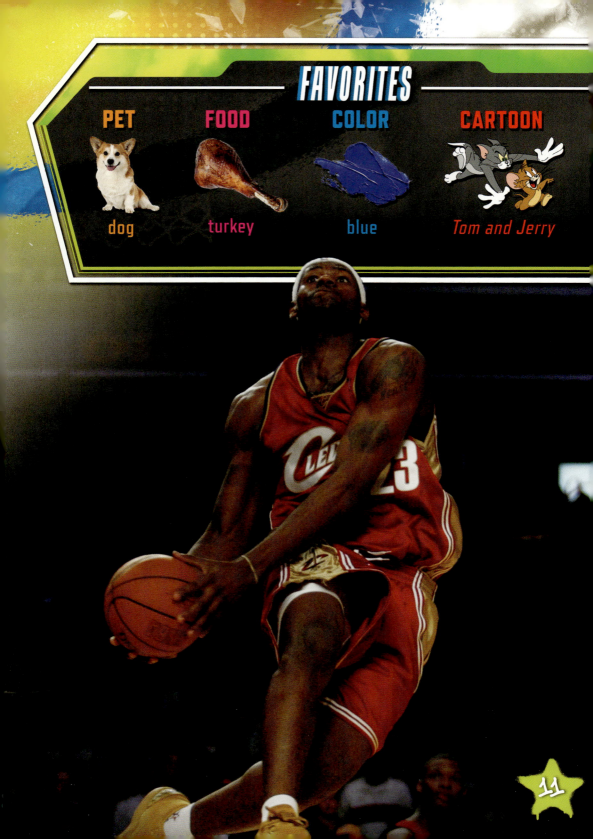

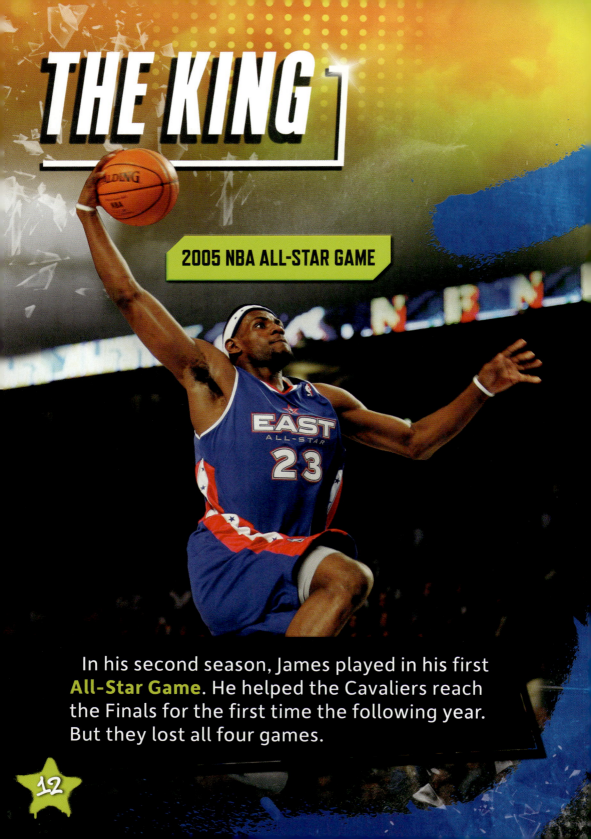

THE KING

2005 NBA ALL-STAR GAME

In his second season, James played in his first **All-Star Game**. He helped the Cavaliers reach the Finals for the first time the following year. But they lost all four games.

In 2008, James led the NBA in scoring. He won the NBA **Most Valuable Player** (MVP) award in 2009 and 2010.

King James

James's nickname is "King James."

2010 NBA MVP

In 2010, James left the Cavaliers. He signed with the Miami Heat. He led the team to the Finals in his first year. But they did not win.

James entered the next season ready to win! He pushed the team to win championships in 2012 and 2013. James was awarded MVP both seasons.

LeBRON JAMES MAP

- **Cleveland Cavaliers, Cleveland, Ohio** — 2003 to 2010, 2014 to 2018
- **Miami Heat, Miami, Florida** — 2010 to 2014
- **Los Angeles Lakers, Los Angeles, California** — 2018 to present

2013 FINALS MVP AND NBA CHAMPION

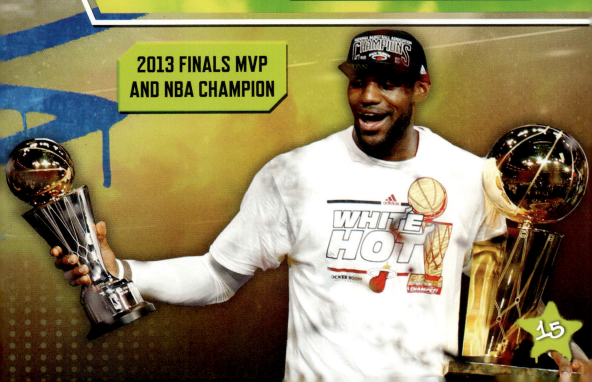

In 2014, James left the Heat. He returned to the Cavaliers. He led the Cavaliers to the Finals. But they lost to the Golden State Warriors.

In 2016, the Cavaliers faced the Warriors again in the Finals. This time they came out on top! James was awarded the Finals MVP for his unbelievable performance.

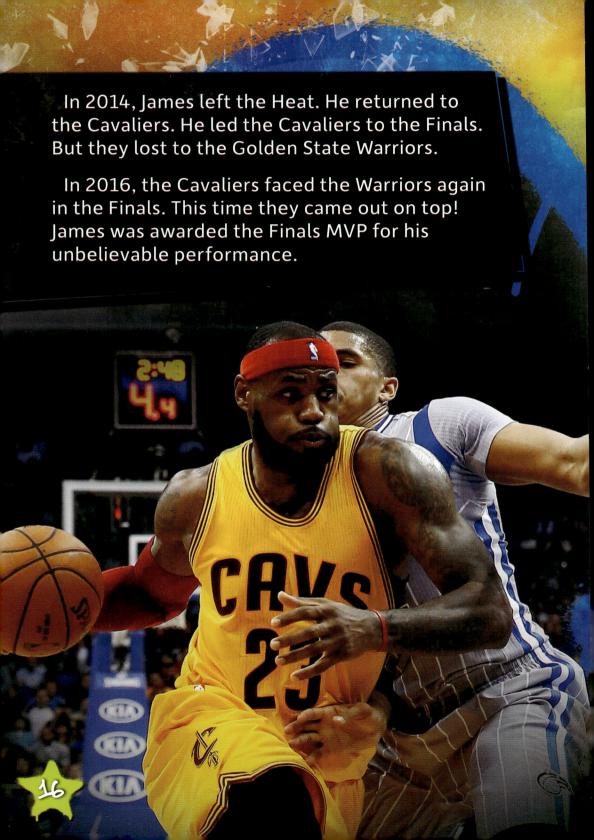

James led the Cavaliers to the Finals two more times. But they lost to the Warriors both times.

In 2018, James signed with the Los Angeles Lakers. He spent much of his first year injured. But James led the Lakers to a championship in 2020!

Welcome to the Jam

James starred in the 2021 film *Space Jam: A New Legacy!*

TIMELINE

— 2003 —
James is drafted by the Cavaliers

— 2010 —
James joins the Heat

— 2012 —
James wins his first championship

— 2014 —
James returns to the Cavaliers

— 2018 —
James joins the Lakers

KING JAMES'S FUTURE

In 2022, James signed a deal to play for the Lakers for two more years. In the future, he plans to play on the same NBA team as his son.

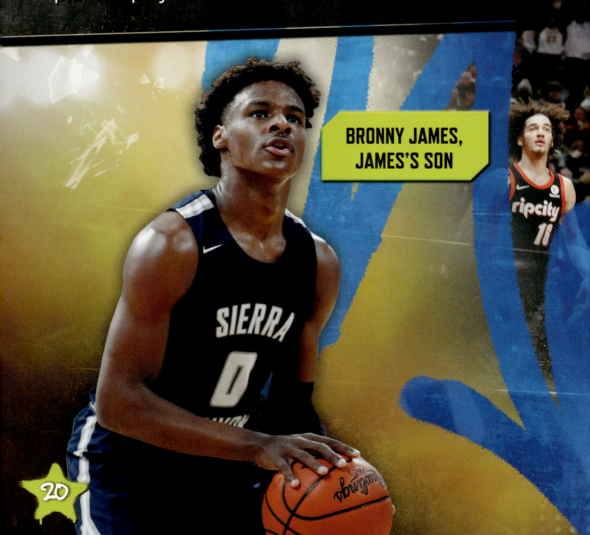

BRONNY JAMES, JAMES'S SON

Team USA

James has played for the United States basketball team in the Olympics. He has won two gold medals and one bronze medal.

LeBron James will likely be in the NBA **Hall of Fame**. But before then he is shooting to win more championships!

GLOSSARY

All-Star Game—a game between the best players in a league

championship—a contest to decide the best team or person

draft—a process during which professional teams choose high school and college players to play for them

Finals—the championship series of the National Basketball Association

Hall of Fame—a place honoring the records of the top people in a sport

most valuable player—the best player in a year, game, or series; the most valuable player is often called the MVP.

National Basketball Association—a professional basketball league in the United States; the National Basketball Association is often called the NBA.

philanthropist—a person who works to help other people

rookie—a first-year player in a sports league

slam dunk—a shot in which a player pushes the basketball forcefully down through the basket

small forward—a position played by a basketball player; small forwards are often the most multiskilled players on the court.

steals—changes in possession when players take the basketball away from players on the other team

TO LEARN MORE

AT THE LIBRARY

Flynn, Brendan. *The Genius Kid's Guide to Pro Basketball.* Mendota Heights, Minn.: North Star Kids, 2022.

Hubbard, Crystal. *Who Is LeBron James?* London, U.K.: Penguin Workshop, 2023.

Wetzel, Dan. *LeBron James.* New York, N.Y.: Henry Holt and Company, 2019.

ON THE WEB

FACTSURFER

Factsurfer.com gives you a safe, fun way to find more information.

1. Go to www.factsurfer.com

2. Enter "LeBron James" into the search box and click 🔍.

3. Select your book cover to see a list of related content.

INDEX

All-Star Game, 12
awards, 9, 10, 13, 14, 15, 16, 17, 21
billionaire, 6
businessman, 7
championship, 4, 8, 14, 15, 18, 21
childhood, 8, 9
Cleveland Cavaliers, 6, 10, 12, 14, 16, 18
draft, 10
favorites, 11
Finals, 4, 12, 14, 15, 16, 17, 18
future, 20, 21
Hall of Fame, 21
Los Angeles Lakers, 4, 6, 18, 20
map, 15
Miami Heat, 6, 14, 16

Most Valuable Player, 13, 14, 15, 16, 17
National Basketball Association, 6, 10, 13, 15, 20, 21
nickname, 13
Nike, 10
Olympics, 21
philanthropist, 7
playing time, 10
profile, 7
Rookie of the Year, 10
scoring, 10, 13
slam dunk, 4, 5
small forward, 6
Space Jam: A New Legacy, 18
steals, 10
timeline, 18–19
trophy shelf, 17

The images in this book are reproduced through the courtesy of: Brian Rothmuller/Icon Sportswir/ APimages, front cover; Dudek1337/ Wiki Commons, p. 3; Douglas P. DeFelice/ Stringer/ Getty Images, pp. 4, 4-5; UPI/ Alamy, p. 6; ZUMA Press/ Alamy, p. 7 (James); JoSte, Snapbacks.cz/ Wiki Commons, p. 7 (Lakers logo); Sporting News Archive/ Contributor/ Getty Images, p. 8; Reuters Photographer/ Alamy, p. 9; Shannon Stapleton/ Alamy, p. 10; Gina Ferazzi/ Contributor/ Getty Images, p. 11; cynoclub, p. 11 (pet); Elena Zajchikova, p. 11 (food); Elena11, p. 11 (color); Sangmesh Desai Darkar, p. 11 (cartoon); Lucy Nicholson/ Alamy, p. 12; Aaron Josefczyk/ Alamy, p. 13; Christian Petersen/ Staff/ Getty Images, p. 14; Ringo Chiu, p. 15 (Los Angeles, California); Adam McCullough, p. 15 (Cleveland, Ohio); pio3, p. 15 (Miami, Florida); Joe Skipper/ Alamy, p. 15 (James); Sam Greenwood/ Staff/ Getty Images, p. 16; San Francisco Chronicle/Hearst Newspapers/ Getty Images, p. 17; Patrick Smith/ Getty Images, pp. 18-19; Mohamed Ahmed Soliman, pp. 18 (2003), 19 (2014); Paulklee1879, p. 18 (2010); Pierre Barlier/ Alamy, p. 19 (2012); Mariyall, p. 19 (2018); Joe Robbins/ Stringer/ Getty Images, p. 20; Steph Chambers/ Staff/ Getty Images, p. 21; Erik Frost/ Wiki Commons, p. 23.